A Voice On The Wind

Nicole Radosti Pipia

Presentation by *BookLeaf Publishing*

Web: www.bookleafpub.com

E-mail: info@bookleafpub.com

ISBN: 9789357214032

First edition 2022

To My Magnificent Husband and Fantastic
Sons

ACKNOWLEDGEMENT

I could not have done this without the loving support of my husband Filippo. He reminded me of what true love is and what it can do. He does so much for our whole family, and asks for nothing in return.

His selflessness and strength will live on in our sons and will brighten this world.

My King, I could never say thank you enough.

I love you always.

PREFACE

I hope this book will bring comfort to those who have gone through similar times. But if nothing else I want to leave something behind that is truly something special to me. My words. So that they might stay with my children and theirs. A connection throughout the years from someone they didn't know, but will always be a part of who they are.

Be Free

Should not the tender of tedious task beware

Of monotony's trance and captor's glare

Passion serenely sets an idle mind free

Revealing the bars, we are not meant to see

But on an inundated mind, despair locks the cage with twist of key.

Do not let this be.

Bickering with buoyant chatter

Shallow and useless clatter.

Content to squabble over likes and praises dropped.

The horizon of thought and wonder cropped.

Seek to learn seek to grow

Otherwise just existing is all you'll ever know

Your Way Home

If I could be found in nature, I would be a
winding path…
One that would always lead you home.
I'd whisper to the wind...
Tell him to step lightly... but quick
For my heart beats louder still…
With yearning thoughts upon your footsteps
heard...
Knock upon my door and find my welcome
Always warm and true.

At Stake

Stories from tattered pages inspire.
Witches' charms and chants said three times
delight.
From within and mirrored above shine bright.
Tempest that is woman to admire.

Stripped to innocence tied to a pyre.
Be silent and accept without fight.
Yield and submit to those of pious might.
To not shed light on truth is dire.

Make it not so our woman's wails be wrought.
Forged not in vain but in pain
Be still.

Here and now so mote it be...onto thee.
For the sorrows and woes, you all have brought.
The emptiness in you our pain won't fill.

Then and now we stand as one, blessed be.

Tempest

Hold me tight again tonight
As the waves of pain crash inside me

Against my shores of reason
Back and forth I feel them ebb and rage
Pressing logic down deep in its watery cage.

It will lose. The chaos anguish causes.

Every time it wails in discontent.
Echoes of wisdom pang against hollow caves of
hurt.
As I call for passion's rise and sorrow's fall.
My heart's waters raging now at the wall.

The tempest above the sea
Cerebral concoctions gust

Reason rains
As wit and patience begin to light the sky
Desire quietly thunders in distancing defiance

The only way to be truly free
Is to know the storm is a part of me

My Sons

You cannot understand my words now little one
They are just sounds and soothing tones
They say I'm your Mama
I'm here, you have nothing to fear. I've got you.
You'll be alright.

You cannot understand my words just yet young
one.
You know some, like ball and play, gonna get
ya, and no...come here, and stay
You know Mommy
It hurts I know... I'm so proud of you...Look at
you go!

You cannot understand my words my little boy
Slow down. Be careful. Be patient. Use your
words.
You know I'm Mommy
I understand. I'm sorry, too. Yes. Five more
minutes.

You cannot understand my words my big boy.
Not yet. That's too much. When you're older.
You know I'm Mom

You know where it counts, in your heart and in
your mind. Have honor. Be kind.

You cannot understand my words young man
Study first. Be careful. Call me. Remember who
you are.
"I know Mom."
I'm proud of the man you've become. Help
others. Be strong.

You cannot understand my words now even
though you're grown
Give them to Grandma. Let me give your wife a
hand. Take some time with each.
"Not right now Mom."
I'm here if you need me. You're doing great with
them. You've made a lovely home.

You cannot understand my words now, they're
just whispers on the wind
Don't cry tears for me. No, don't argue about
that. Be there for each other.
"We miss you Mom"
Sweet boy...even though I'm not near, you have
nothing to fear. It hurts I know, but I'm so very
proud of you. I understand, and I'm sorry. I wish
we had five more minutes too. Remember where
it counts. I was always proud to be your mom.

To Know Rage

No. You're annoyed. I see your eyes roll and
watch you heave a heavy sigh.
No. You're frustrated. I hear your groans and see
your furrowing brow.
No. You're angry. I see your fists clenched from
a quick temper. Your face flushed.
No.
You don't know the rage I know.
The terrible pulsing within your chest. The wails
that you can't control.
They thunder around you. Your chest heaving
Caving in.
Breaths deepening.
The shattering of your heart
Your very soul.
For rage comes when someone you love is
hurting
And it's beyond our control.
Our hands tied, even as we set the binds to burn.
No. You don't know rage like I do.
And I hope you never do.
But if you find yourself there.
You're not alone.
We are as wolves howling at the moon.
Our souls laid bare.

Silent Embrace

My heart soars beyond the treetops.
Searching for only the stars that can guide my
weary eyes tonight.
The stillness of the night, a silent embrace of
understanding.
My purpose to ground and guide those by my
side.
I cannot waver less all will be lost.

A hold within my hands the tethers tied to each
of you.
But as time yields lavish lengths of sturdy
rope...all are still firmly anchored to my heart.
You pull proud and strong, my burdens lighten
When all of your courses marry and are merry
beneath your feet.

But do you not see that when you fight and
taught and begrudge
Your strength and your unruly pride
Tear
It will be the very death of me.

For I will never pull up the anchor.
I will never leave you without hold.

For by my life or by my death I will hold you to
each other

You Set Me Free

I've loved you. But I never thought my heart
could truly love in full again. I felt there was a
damn on my heart. A stony curse that wouldn't
allow my passions to flow.
Because of the barren desert I let my soul
become.
The treachery that reeked havoc upon me down
to the roots
It left me bereft of hope and my heart barren.

I've always loved you but now I feel the dam is
gone.
My love runs and rushes through me
Filling every inch
With lush and vibrant life.
As hope inside me looks towards the distant hills
You stand there knee deep in rushing waters.
Ax in hand, with a knowing smile.
"Those walls have stood long enough around
your heart I think. You've no need for them. I've
torn them down."
I smile back as the cool misty spray brushes my
cheeks. My warrior doesn't fear to drown in the
strength of my rushing and rising tides.

I've always loved you, but because of you, I can
love you without reserve
For my love for you will never run dry.
What we've both been waiting for
and so deserve

When You Both Leave

My heart quakes and shatters into a million
pieces the very second and every time you both
leave.

Hope of when we'll be together again shines
through the pain to prick holes in a darkening
night sky.

My king knows and helps reform the well
known puzzle of my heart strewn upon our floor.

He takes his place by my side
Awaiting you both at our door

Take A Moment

Father Time...please
Just a bit..
Let me sit here
Sip my coffee
And think
My thoughts rise
Along the horizon of my still sleepy mind
The dawn takes a seat beside me in kind
Her warm embrace surrounds
The birds chirp just beyond the pane
A moment one could easily just miss
If a to-do playlist roared over the bliss
Thank you Father Time for the glimpse that
made me be still
Taking this gift for granted I never will

See Yourself

I want to write about that time
Truth be told it happened once or twice
I was young
Had just been so calm
At ease and without any thought

I saw myself, through eyes
On the outside looking in

A cinematic wide shot
Of glorious splendor

What I know now, that I didn't know then
Was how close I had come to my own personal
zen
I've since searched to have this moment and in
vain, for every attempt to settle my mind busies
it
Again and again

I had become the world around me and felt such
release
Understood and felt the depth of it all
Found such peace

Realized my part in it was so insignificantly
small

It didn't make me panic
Or feel sad

It made me realize how important each breath
Each action
Each word

Running parallel beside our subconscious
collective connection
Far from trivial
A potential so pivotal

I will never stop
I try almost every day
I hope to find the way

Why We Teach

I'm sure it will follow that I once taught
Got up early weekday mornings
Learned my students names
Graded papers, planned lessons, and help friends
do the same

But over the years, and as the world changed
The essays, the word problems, the standards,
the common core...
The world grew cold, and there was something
my students always needed more...

I gave out tissues, tied ten dozen shoes
Zipped up jackets, so many flus!
Fixed broken backpacks so they could make it
one more trip home

Listened to stories from voices too often
silenced
Baked the only cupcakes certain birthdays
would see
Brought in clothes for concerts, and gave them
out secretly
Gave hugs in silence when I didn't have the
words

Cried together when words just weren't enough

Prepared and shared a closet for
Monthly monsters who would pay a surprise
visit
Arm wrestles had to rally the rousers
and gain their respect
Allowed myself to laugh and learn
As they needed to teach someone...they taught
me in turn

Helped some bring their walls down
While showing others how to put'em up
Helped friends learn how to mend bonds and say
sorry
Helped enemies disagree, but do so respectfully

Endless field trip head counts, lunch detention
pouts...
CPS calls, scrubbing pain off bathroom stall
walls
Not backing down when they needed someone
around
Being their fifth man so they could play...
Even though that meant extra traffic that day

Taking the hard questions even when I was
afraid

I didn't always have the answer but I led with
my heart
Whether they were gay, led astray, lost their
way, or if their anger made them pay
I didn't judge them I held them
Some I told so much
Some were told the same thing so many times
But to others only a few things here and there...

Be kind
Think before you speak
There's nothing wrong with not liking someone
but be respectful
Stand up for yourself
You chose what you want out of life
Seek happiness inside yourself and gain it their
first
You are responsible for your actions and your
words
Let your choices weigh heavy on you or the
consequences will weigh more

I hope for even just one..
That I made their days a little brighter
Their smiles last a little longer
Their sadnesses not so strong

Yes I taught. But I learned all along.

My King

Thank you
I know there is little for me you wouldn't do

You'll move a mountain to fetch me a flower
Gaze under the stars hour after hour

I don't really know if you will ever know
How much you've done for me
It would only be through my eyes
That you could truly see

Forgiveness

The silence is deafening after my heart cries out in pain. How could I have been so stupid. How could I have been so naive? Making the same mistakes...hoping for the same foolish dream. Can it ever go back to the beautiful innocence it once was? How could the clouds take back the rain?

Little Moments

In the stillness of the morning laying next to my
sons I find peace.

All three
Leaning on me
Their bodies still
Save the small breaths that make their chests rise
and fall ever so slightly.

Their little noses. Soft little toes. My love for
them just grows and grows.

He Came For Me

I'm awake this morning after dreaming of you.

You came to me in a dream but long ago

Rescuing me then, like you have now

Not just from dangers but from myself

I've worked so hard to find the love I've found
in you

But now that I have you

I no longer know if I'm good enough

Sometimes I feel like there's nothing left to me
Nothing left to be good enough to hold onto you

I've been through a war and don't know what
it's like to be at peace.

I fell like my heart is in ruins my soul laid bare

With each step I take towards you
I take towards what once was me too

A distant but not forsaken memory

I don't see yet what you say you see
When you look at me

But something inside of me hears your voice
telling me to get up…
Rise Up
Above the ashes surrounding you
You command.
See
You've burnt you've survived. You've fought so
hard to live
Breath in the free air
You are reborn

Hope

Kindness is never an act of wasted effort.
It gives wings to hope.

Hope's flight
A perilous and fragile one.
A journey of cause, consequence, resolve, and
rebirth.

Anger, jealousy, rage, and hatred
All distractions of the mind that we create
Allow others to make us feel
In order to mislead us
Far away and astray from the truth and
happiness we had set out to find.

This has become life's labyrinth
As all the people in the world are stuck
and have succumb to life's laboring distractions.
Truth, justice, and good buried deep beneath the
rubble
Of a world tearing itself apart.
Hope a battered bird now ambling amidst the
debris.

But I will see the battered bird reborn now
Like a phoenix from the ashes and with it
The good in this world.

The Moutain

The wind does howl
The mountain must never bow
The wind just moves by

Fibonacci on a Sunday Morning

Love
Binds
It Heals
Bonds due yield
Brings wind to the sail
Calms the seas of a lonely heart

Lessons Forged

My anger is an ancient sword
Forged in the flames of your depression
Sharpened by your distain

He taught me to lift a blade
Explained how to carry it and stand

I cut myself when your words sharpened the tip

His wisdom became its sheath

Instead of an embrace your distant arms armed
me against the worlds upcoming distaste

The world that needs, but doesn't always accept
Those who come so heavily armed

I can't change who I am

From my pain purpose took its first breath

I would rather die by the blade in my hand
Then to watch swords be drawn
By the hands of my sons

They will never know a banished land
They can always find my arms

He's left me now too
Like you

But the lessons stay
From you both
I've found my way

Forgiveness replaces anger
Hurt gives way to kind

You taught me
How not to be

At the Close

Rest your head until the dawn
Another day will come
Despite the darkness and the night

We are of the light
No matter what you face or your burden
It can't last

Harness the the strength of day's promise to
return
Let the embers of salvation breath
Your inner peace will catch and burn

For sorrow and suffering are all in your
perspective
It's true
Your happiness must always be found in you

Mind and heart need not always agree, but must
exist in harmony
Let all of what you are and do align
Even as the longest nights set in

Honor the promise
Be the dawn